ideals

THANKSGIVING ISSUE

There's a joyful calm to the autumn time
When we fall in step with the season's rhyme,
As the sun shines forth with a golden glow
And when nature puts on a beauty show,
Then the grapes have turned to a purple hue
And the sky is dyed a celestial blue,
Till the west is splashed with a crimson streak
And the wine drops circle the apple's cheek,
When the bins are stacked with a wealth of grain,
Ah, the autumn days have too short a reign.

Ray I. Hoppman

Editorial Director, James Kuse
Managing Editor, Ralph Luedtke
Photographic Editor, Gerald Koser
Production Editor, Stuart L. Zyduck

designed by
Colleen Callahan Gonring
and
Jan Frances Engel

Color

Have you noticed, have you seen
That God loves green?
And that he loves clear yellow, too,
And blue—blue!
The trees, the sky, the glint of the sun,
The million yellow flowers that run
Their windy way;
And God loves gray:
The mist, the rain, the clouds that fly
When storms go by.
And looking at the dawn, I think
That God loves pink.
But red—have you ever thought how He
Uses it so sparingly?
A red flower here, another there,
A red wing flashing on the air,
A cluster of berries on a limb—
Red must be jewel-like to Him,
And very precious—but if I
Were asked the color I like best
'Twould be the color of the sky
Some autumn evening in the west:
Not mauve, not pink, not gold, not flame—
It has no name!

Grace Noll Crowell

"Color" by Grace Noll Crowell, From POEMS OF INSPIRA-
TION AND COURAGE by Grace Noll Crowell. Copyright 1946
by Harper & Row, Publishers, Inc. Reprinted by permission of
the publisher.

IDEALS—Vol. 35, No. 5—September 1978. Published bimonthly by IDEALS PUBLISHING CORPORATION, 11315 Watertown Plank Road,
Milwaukee, Wis. 53226. Second-class postage paid at Milwaukee, Wisconsin © 1978 by IDEALS PUBLISHING CORPORATION.
All rights reserved. Title IDEALS registered U.S. Patent Office.
ONE YEAR SUBSCRIPTION—six consecutive issues as published—only $10.00
TWO YEAR SUBSCRIPTION—twelve consecutive issues as published—only $17.00
SINGLE ISSUES—only $2.50

ISBN 0-89542-316-2 250

Photograph Opposite
Freelance Photographers Guild

September

I found September smiling there, beneath a sky of blue,
A halo made of goldenrod and shining fresh with dew,
I loved the cricket's evening song, the day's last golden glow,
The quiet breeze among the leaves that seemed to sparkle so.

I found a melancholy heart, as summer lingered there,
Not ready yet to bid farewell, though stay she mustn't dare,
Old Mister Frost so near at hand, in orchard, field and glen,
The sun to steal a final glow, then on its way again.

I'll keep September dear to me,
As autumn wears away,
And through tomorrow I shall have
A mem'ry of today;
The lovely flowers quite faded now,
Yet fragrant, it would seem
September in her final days
Still does rule supreme.

I loved September's shining hours,
And thrilled to evenings cool
The youngsters that she took from play
And started off to school,
And though she's never long enough,
Too quickly come and gone,
September is a golden month
That lives right on and on.

Garnett Ann Schultz

The Art of Fleurage

No, you won't find fleurage in the dictionary. It's a word coined by artist Harry White of Jamaica Plain, Massachusetts, to describe his work and his art. What then is fleurage? It's simply pressing flowers—and then creating a floral masterpiece.

A fleurage is begun by pressing flowers or, as in the case of roses, iris or daffodils, pressing single petals. Do this by separating and spreading the petals of the flowers, then placing them between paper-lined pages of large phone books, library dictionaries, or smaller books with a heavy weight on top.

The paper used to line the book acts as a blotter in the drying process and the texture of the paper will affect the look of the dried petals. For instance, paper towels transfer their pattern to the surface of soft rose petals. Interesting effects can be obtained in this way, but for a smooth petal, or a natural-looking one, use soft facial tissue as a blotter.

Place the books in a warm, dry place and in about two weeks the petals will be dried and can be used. They become like paper, and fleurage can be thought of as creating a collage from petals.

When Harry White constructs his fleurage, he begins by outlining his design with pencil on a smooth surface, such as four-ply museum board, clean glass, or wood. He then fills in the outlined areas by glueing on the petals. A nonacid white glue is the best adhesive for this. Because Harry wants his fleurages to last, he uses the same adhesive libraries use to bind antique books.

The remaining work involved in creating a fleurage is really up to the individual and is "the art" of fleurage. Harry uses whole petals, cuts them with an exacto blade, or even tears them to achieve the effect he is looking for. He paints some with glue then presses them to the surface; whereas other petals are so delicate that he applies glue to the board and then presses on the petals. Some of the more delicate petals are those of the iris which will shrivel upon contact with moisture. With these petals, speed is important, and planning ahead is essential.

The petals in a fleurage will fade, but this process often enhances the overall effect and beauty of the work. The finished product should not, however, be hung where the sun will reach it as it will fade faster. Treat a fleurage as you would a fine watercolor and it will last for years.

Fleurage is a unique art requiring practice and a familiarity with flowers. More importantly, it is a way of preserving the beauty of summer all year through.

Fleurage Design Opposite
JOURNEY OF THE SUN
Harry R. White
Photo, Stein Studios, Inc.

The Dignity of Labor

Our God and Creator, Thou hast created man in Thine image, endowing him with creative powers. Thou hast given him a resourceful mind and skillful hands wherewith he can dominate the world of nature; he can unlock its pent-up powers and make them serve his every want. We thank Thee, O God, for the capacity to work wherein men are different from all other living beings.

For these others survive by adjusting themselves to their environment, but man has survived by transforming his environment and adjusting it to himself. Grant that we may never abuse those powers that give dignity to our work, that we may ever remember that our creativity is Thy gift, designed for Thy service, and that, when our plans conform not to Thy designs, the structures we create collapse over our heads. Give us the humility and the wisdom to employ our labors only to just ends, to purposes from which all can benefit and from which none will suffer hurt. Check in us the greed of acquisition and the lust of domination, that we may all enjoy the fruits of our toil without denying to any the fruits of theirs. Let us never forget our dependence on one another and on that spirit of brotherhood which is a manifestation of Thy love. For each of us by himself is weak and helpless, and only our cooperation makes our work effective.

The tools that we use, the knowledge that we apply, the very bread that we eat, are not of our single creation but are the accumulated product of the toil and skill of many workers over many generations. Inspire us, therefore, with loyalty to all who work and with the spirit of mutual helpfulness and brotherly love.

Give us the strength to produce abundantly, the justice to distribute equitably, and the wisdom and self-control to consume prudently the goods that satisfy our needs, that we may all know the joy of creativity, the thrill of comradeship, the zest of health, and the peace of mind that are the reward of human labor when it conforms with Thy divine will.

The First Day of School

The little country school, fast passing away,
Is now just a memory of yesterday.
How happy the times which many recall,
When school days again returned with the fall.

When the first day arrived we hardly could wait
To start off to school with our books and our slates.
We tripped down the road, so happy and gay,
And each home recruited along the way.

From beginners, called chart class, to eighth grade, as a rule,
All were taught by one teacher in the country school.
At the sound of the handbell, how we did run
Into the schoolhouse. Then school had begun.

Turn back the pages, let memory recall
A time when you started back to school in the fall.
Those fond recollections in memory held fast,
Bring to mind happy school days we had in the past.

Ottis Shirk

The Huskers

It was late in mild October,
and the long autumnal rain
Had left the summer harvest-fields
all green with grass again;
The first sharp frosts had fallen,
leaving all the woodlands gay
With the hues of summer's rainbow,
or the meadow-flowers of May.

Through a thin, dry mist, that morning,
the sun rose broad and red,
At first a rayless disk of fire,
he brightened as he sped;
Yet even his noontide glory
fell chastened and subdued,
On the cornfields and the orchards
and softly pictured wood.

And all that quiet afternoon,
slow sloping to the night,
He wove with golden shuttle
the haze with yellow light;
Slanting through the painted beeches,
he glorified the hill;
And, beneath it, pond and meadow
lay brighter, greener still.

And shouting boys in woodland haunts
caught glimpses of that sky,
Flecked by the many-tinted leaves,
and laughed, they knew not why;
And school-girls, gay with aster-flowers,
beside the meadow brooks,
Mingled the glow of autumn
with the sunshine of sweet looks.

From spire and barn looked westerly
the patient weathercocks;
But even the birches on the hill
stood motionless as rocks.
No sound was in the woodlands,
save the squirrel's dropping shell,
And the yellow leaves among the boughs,
low rustling as they fell.

The summer grains were harvested;
the stubble-fields lay dry,
Where June winds rolled, in light and shade,
the pale green waves of rye;
But still, on gentle hill-slopes,
in valleys fringed with wood,
Ungathered, bleaching in the sun,
the heavy corn crop stood.

Bent low, by autumn's wind and rain,
through husks that, dry and sere,
Unfolded from their ripened charge,
shone out the yellow ear;
Beneath the turnip lay concealed,
in many a verdant fold,
And glistened in the slanting light
the pumpkin's sphere of gold.

There wrought the busy harvesters;
and many a creaking wain
Bore slowly to the long barn-floor
its load of husk and grain;
Till broad and red, as when he rose,
the sun sank down, at last,
And like a merry guest's farewell,
the day in brightness passed.

And lo! as through the western pines,
on meadow, stream, and pond,
Flamed the red radiance of a sky,
set all afire beyond,
Slowly o'er the eastern sea-bluffs
a milder glory shone,
And the sunset and the moonrise
were mingled into one!

As thus into the quiet night
the twilight lapsed away,
And deeper in the brightening moon
the tranquil shadows lay;
From many a brown old farm-house,
and hamlet without name,
Their milking and their home-tasks done,
the merry huskers came.

Swung o'er the heaped-up harvest,
from pitchforks in the mow,
Shone dimly down the lanterns
on the pleasant scene below;
The growing pile of husks behind,
the golden ears before,
And laughing eyes and busy hands
and brown cheeks glimmering o'er.

Half hidden, in a quiet nook,
serene of look and heart,
Talking their old times over,
the old men sat apart;
While up and down the unhusked pile,
or nestling in its shade,
At hide-and-seek, with laugh and shout,
the happy children played.

Urged by the good host's daughter,
a maiden young and fair,
Lifting to light her sweet blue eyes
and pride of soft brown hair,
The master of the village school,
sleek of hair and smooth of tongue,
To the quaint tune of some old psalm,
a husking-ballad sung.

John Greenleaf Whittier

The Wind and the Leaves

"Come, little leaves," said the wind one day,
"Come o'er the meadows with me and play;
Put on your dresses of red and gold—
For summer is gone and the days grow cold."

Soon as the leaves heard the wind's loud call,
Down they came fluttering, one and all;
Over the brown fields they danced and flew,
Singing the soft little songs they knew.

"Cricket, goodby, we've been friends so long,
Little brook, sing us your farewell song;
Say you are sorry to see us go;
Ah! you will miss us, right well we know.

"Dear little lambs, in your fleecy fold,
Mother will keep you from harm and cold;
Fondly we watched you in vale and glade,
Say, will you dream of our loving shade?"

Dancing and whirling, the little leaves went,
Winter had called them, and they were content;
Soon fast asleep in their earthly beds,
The snow laid a coverlet over their heads.

George Cooper

Hours of Bliss

Oh, may these eyes of mine
    be clear and open wide
To view the beauty round about
    that makes today divine;
To see the diamonds on the grass
    made by the morning mist;
And two butterflies who pass
    by a bloom to sneak a kiss.

To see the thriving pumpkins,
    still green with streaks of yellow,
Before their big night comes
    and they turn orange and mellow;
To watch the honeybees
    suck the sweetness of a pear
That ripened and fell
    before the picker was there.

Oh, may these ears of mine
    hear every hushed and soothing sound:
The purring of a kitten,
    the yawn of a dosing hound;
The rustling of the cornstalks
    as a breeze stirs by;
The song a bird remembers
    and warbles forth with a sigh.

And hear the crackling of a bonfire
    on an autumn day;
The fluttering of leaves, the rustling,
    as a rake is put into play;
The swishing of a busy broom
    against a backporch step;
And the pattering of children's feet
    running out to play and full of pep!

The simple, tender, common scenes
    that make a day like this,
And the hushed sweet song September sings
    provides me with these hours of bliss!

Joy Belle Burgess

Lord, Bless This House

Lord, bless this house and bless us all
In care and pleasure, great or small;
Blest be the door friends enter by,
And windows that let in the sky,
And roof above and walls about
That shut the world and weather out!
Lord, make my house a mansion of
Abiding loveliness and love,
A friendly, comfortable place.
Let pleasant talk like firelight grace
These rooms, and may friends linger long
To join in laughter or a song.
Blest be these rooms for work or play!
Oh, let my house be sometimes gay
And sometimes still as candlelight.
Be with us, Lord, both day and night;
Blest be our labor and our rest;
Our waking and our sleep be blest.
In care and pleasure, great or small,
Lord, bless this house and bless us all!

James Dillet Freeman

Photograph Opposite
Robert Cushman Hayes

John Greenleaf Whittier

John Greenleaf Whittier is best remembered as a balladeer and poet of the romantic, everyday American life of the mid-nineteenth century. For most of his life, however, he was the radical and reformer, the pacifist and preacher. Whittier's first poem, "The Exile's Departure," was published in the *Newburyport Free Press*, an anti-slavery newspaper. For the next thirty years, Whittier was a vocal abolitionist, involved in propaganda and politics, and, in 1834, a state senator. Only after the passage of the Emancipation Proclamation did Whittier consistently turn to the common and the rural for his subjects. At the age of fifty-eight, he wrote his most popular poem, "Snow-Bound." By now, the strident reformer had become the harmless balladeer and the dire radical a gentle poet.

The Last Walk in Autumn

O'er the bare woods,
Whose outstretched hands
Plead with the leaden heavens in vain,
I see, beyond the valley lands,
The sea's long level dim with rain.
Around me all things, stark and dumb,
Seem praying for the snows to come,
And, for the summer bloom
And greenness gone,
With winter's sunset lights
And dazzling morn atone.

I passed this way a year ago:
The wind blew south; the noon of day
Was warm as June's; and save that snow
Flecked the low mountains far away,
And that the vernal-seeming breeze
Mocked faded grass and leafless trees,
I might have dreamed of summer as I lay,
Watching the fallen leaves
With the soft wind at play.

Selection

Heap high the farmer's wintry hoard!
　Heap high the golden corn!
No richer gift has Autumn poured
　From out her lavish horn.

Let other lands exulting glean
　The apple from the pine,
The orange from its glossy green,
　The cluster from the vine,

But let the good old corn adorn
　The hills our fathers trod;
Still let us, for His golden corn,
　Send up our thanks to God.

Seed-Time and Harvest

As o'er his furrowed fields which lie
Beneath a coldly-dropping sky,
Yet chill with winter's melted snow,
The husbandman goes forth to sow,

Thus, Freedom, on the bitter blast
The ventures of thy seed we cast,
And trust to warmer sun and rain
To swell the germ, and fill the grain.

Who calls thy glorious service hard?
Who deems it not its own reward?
Who, for its trials, counts it less
A cause of praise and thankfulness?

It may not be our lot to wield
The sickle in the ripened field;
Nor ours to hear, on summer eves,
The reaper's song among the sheaves.

Yet where our duty's task is wrought
In unison with God's great thought,
The near and future blend in one,
And whatsoe'er is willed, is done!

And ours the grateful service whence
Comes, day by day, the recompense;
The hope, the trust, the purpose stayed,
The fountain and the noonday shade.

And were this life the utmost span,
The only end and aim of man,
Better the toil of fields like these
Than waking dream and slothful ease.

But life, though falling like our grain,
Like that revives and springs again;
And, early called, how blest are they
Who wait in heaven their harvest-day.

God sought to describe gentleness,
And so a doe was born;
He thought of pride and fashioned
A lordly anchored stag;
And to explain the word called grace,
He made a dappled fawn.

One dusk, by a river's edge,
I chanced to glimpse pride,
Gentleness and grace
Caught, deep in tree shadows,
Drinking of the cool
River waters.

Heather Kirkwood

H. Crane

I think I could turn and live with the animals,
    they are so placid and self-contain'd,
        I stand and look at them long and long.

Walt Whitman

GRANDMOTHERS
GRANDFATHERS

randmother,
randfather!
Sent from above;
Child-hugging, heart-tugging, symbols
   of love!
Kind, understanding faith that supplies
You who are keepers of family ties.

randmother,
randfather!
Life is a test.
You are the guardian of all that is best.
Teacher, example, leader of men,
Someone who listens, wonderful friend!

Days become special when shared
   with a child.
Grandmother sits with them, family
   style.
Time to teach lessons with afternoon
   teas,
Calling on neighbors, trying to please.

Rainy days spent with a "memory"
   trunk,
Making real treasures from discarded
   junk.
Sharing their secrets, finding their toys,
Teaching them gently life's special joys.

Knit a warm sweater, make pinafores,
Sewing and cooking, shopping in stores,
Note the resemblance to Mother and
   Dad,
Flooded with memories, refreshing
   and glad.
Cookies need baking, swings need a
   shove,
Grandmothers know the importance of
   love.

randfathers,
randmothers!
    Yours to enjoy,
Play with and daydream
With your girl or boy!
Grandfathers whistle, sometimes they
    talk,
Tell a good story, go for a walk.

Go along fishing with someone who
    cares,
Yelling at ballgames, listening to
    prayers.
Deep down inside, the heart sings a
    song,
Feeling like springtime, vibrant and
    strong!
Grandchildren grow up too fast to
    measure.
Grandfathers know they are something
    to treasure.
randmother,
randfather!
    Hold out your hand!
For this you were chosen, a part of
    God's plan,
To love them, to lead them, remove
    doubt and fear.
Tomorrow is present when children are
    near!

John Goodman

GRANDPARENTS' DAY

Did you know that Grandparents' Day, not unlike the traditional Mother's and Father's days, is celebrated in the state of Massachusetts? As far as we know, it is one of the few states in which the day is observed, but wouldn't it be wonderful, and certainly deserving, if Grandparents' Day were to be celebrated on a national level. If you share our feeling, please drop us a line c/o Ideals Publishing Corporation, The Grandparents' Day Committee, 11315 Watertown Plank Road, Milwaukee, Wis. 53201.

You can be assured your letters and cards will be noted, counted and presented to the people who can help us establish Grandparents' Day.

September Comes in Quietly

September comes in quietly at Stillmeadow. The gardens in the valley are in full bloom. Sunlight sifts through the canopy of the giant maples—as it has all summer. The pond water is as clear and dark as if it had been polished.

And yet I go out one morning and know that summer is drifting up the hill in the soft blue haze. And I feel an urgency to gather in all the loveliness of the past blazing days and star-cool nights and keep them forever. But fall is here. Goldenrod is splashing color along the road, and wild asters open their delicate amethyst petals. In the swamp, the first scarlet burns above the huckleberry bushes.

Days grow shorter now, and the first frost will come midmonth. Migrant birds leave according to their own mysterious schedule. Squirrels fling themselves from tree to tree in a burst of activity. I always hope they store enough hickory nuts and acorns, but they never do. What they do is to eat the bird food from the feeders.

The woodchucks are busy, too. Now and then an overstuffed one gets in the road and is run down, but not by me. And there is no shooting done on my acres except when the children bang away at a tomato can nailed to a post. So the wild people can go about their business as I go about mine.

Now that so much of the woodlands has been destroyed, I sometimes wonder just how many dwellers there are in my woods and swamps. Most of the deer have gone, and this is a sad loss. The movement of a deer is like a madrigal, and a wobbly fawn adds a grace note.

There are many things to do before the long cold sets in, but it is so easy to put them off. For this is a dreaming time and a time to be thankful. I do not want to miss the beauty of moonlight dipping into the pond, or the smell of wild grapes by the gray stone fence, or the sound of a katydid singing the requiem of summer.

Gladys Taber

Photograph Opposite
lance Photographers Guild

Little Orphant Annie

James Whitcomb Riley

Little Orphant Annie's come to our house to stay,
An' wash the cups and saucers up, an' brush the crumbs away,
An' shoo the chickens off the porch, an' dust the hearth, an' sweep,
An' make the fire, an' bake the bread, an' earn her board-an'-keep;
An' all us other children, when the supper things is done,
We set around the kitchen fire an' has the mostest fun
A-lis'nin' to the witch-tales 'at Annie tells about,
An' the Gobble-uns 'at gits you
        Ef you
          Don't
            Watch
            Out!

An' one time a little girl 'ud allus laugh an' grin,
An' make fun of ever'one, an' all her blood-an'-kin;
An' onc't when they was "company," an' ole folks was there,
She mocked 'em an' shocked 'em, an' said she didn't care!
An' thist as she kicked her heels, an' turn't to run an' hide,
They was two great big Black Things a-standin' by her side,
An' they snatched her through the ceilin' 'fore she knowed what she's about!
An' the Gobble-uns 'll git you
        Ef you
          Don't
            Watch
            Out!

Onc't they was a little boy wouldn't say his pray'rs—
An' when he went to bed at night, away up stairs,
His mammy heered him holler, an' his daddy heard him bawl,
An' when they turn't the kivvers down, he wasn't there at all!
An' they seeked him in the rafter-room, an' cubby-hole, an' press,
An' seeked him up the chimney-flue, an' ever'wheres, I guess;
But all they ever found was thist his pants an' round-about!
An' the Gobble-uns 'll git you
        Ef you
          Don't
            Watch
            Out!

An' little Orphant Annie says, when the blaze is blue,
An' the lampwick sputters, an' the wind goes woo-oo!
An' you hear the crickets quit, an' the moon is gray,
An' the lightnin'-bugs in dew is all squenched away,—
You better mind yer parents, and yer teachers fond and dear,
An' cherish them 'at loves you, an' dry the orphant's tear,
An' he'p the pore an' needy ones 'at clusters all about,
Er the Gobble-uns 'll git you

Ef you
Don't
Watch
Out!

GOLDEN DAYS of Autumn

These glorious, hazy, golden days of autumn—
    of Indian summer—
        shall pass all too soon.

The foot-crunching leaves will be silent,
    the multicolored leaves
        fallen and covered.

Already the mountaintops have been dipped
    in the ice cream of our harshest season,
        while the high peaks echo to the bugling elk.

He knows instinctively that he must soon forage
    beneath the heavy white blanket
        which will insulate the earth.

But if winter comes, as it surely must,
    the spring shall follow also, bringing life again
        to the earth in different shades of green.

Some of us will see again those glorious, hazy,
    golden days of yet another autumn.

William H. Kemp

ON A PORTRAIT OF COLUMBUS

Was this his face, and these the finding eyes
That plucked a new world from the rolling seas?
Who, serving Christ, whom most he sought to please,
Willed his one thought until he saw arise

Man's other home and earthly paradise—
His early vision, when with stalwart knees
He pushed the boat from his young olive-trees;
And sailed to wrest the secret of the skies.

He on the waters dared to set his feet,
And through believing planted earth's last race.
What faith in man must in our new world beat,
Thinking how once he saw before his face
The west and all the host of stars retreat
Into the silence infinite of space!

George S. Woodberry

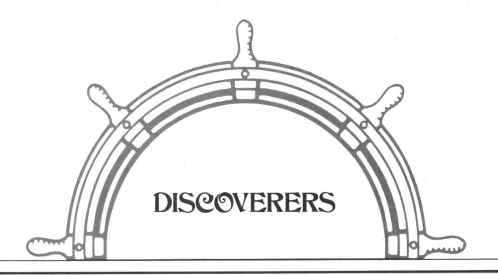

DISCOVERERS

Since ever earth knew man, his heart was dreaming
Of some millennial and promised shore.
Each one has had that westward vision, gleaming
Upon his fancy; like a city seeming,
That summons evermore.

Those cloud-capped towers, built by man's soul unaided,
On solid earth leave not a rack behind,
But, like an unsubstantial pageant faded,
Melt into air, thin air, by visions raided,
The cities of his mind.

We, still discoverers over stormy breakers,
Must build our vision-city as we may,
Kept mindful of our fathers, those old makers
Of history, of beaten trails forsakers
Whose hopes are roads today.

Man's soul is a discoverer, pioneering,
His bark is set upon an unknown sea,
And, with its white sail by the high stars steering,
The great Discovery is ever nearing,
The one Land of the Free.

Isabel Fiske Conant

Night of Enchantment

On this night of fun and frolic,
Beneath a yellow moon,
A spell of strange enchantment
Veils every mask and witch's broom;

For when nightfall shrouds the lane,
Eerie forms are heard and seen
As they dart amid the shadows
To scare little spooks on Halloween!

Ghosts and goblins find delight
In haunting midst the shade of gloom,
While witches shriek their wildest cries
From high aloft on flying brooms.

The black cat slinks along the fence
And stops to hiss and scowl,
And fir trees hide within their boughs
A pair of hooting owls;

But still the bravest of all spooks
Skip gaily down the lane,
And smile at every jack-o'-lantern
Glowing from a windowpane.
On this night of fun and frolic,
Beneath a yellow moon,
The spell of strange enchantment ends,
For little spooks, too soon!

Joy Belle Burgess

Photograph Oppo
Ralph Luedtke

Autumn Tapestry

Weave me a hanging
        with bold rustic thread.
Fly me some geese
        in a V overhead.
Toss some red berries
        on a carpet of leaves,
Send milkweed sailing
        like chutes on the breeze.
Glisten brown cattails
        with diamonds of dew,
Sunbeam the clouds;
        Let the heavens shine through.

Fill some small shuttles
        with dark shades of green,
Spread with a flair
        giving life to the scene.
Frost up the brook
        but leave her sweet tune.
Give me a glimpse
        of the big harvest moon.
Splash some bright orange
        by the tall shocks of corn.
Show just a part
        of a new harvest moon.

Finish with fringes
        of God's love and care.
Hang it with grace:
        It's my Thanksgiving prayer!

Alice Leedy Mason

Signs and Wonders

Autumn is in the air once more,
Bright hills are all aflame.
   The cricket sings
   Of warmer things.
Earth's no longer the same.

Green leaves have turned to gold again,
Wild birds sail the sky,
   The new frost nips
   And the night wind whips.
Sun wears a glint in his eye.

Meadows beyond the old stone fence
Are lovely, near and far.
   They seem to hold
   That touch of gold,
Bright as an autumn star.

Rich color changes hill and glen,
Wild sumac shows its fire.
   True beauty starts
   To lift all hearts
Like amens from a choir.

Grateful hearts give thanks to God
For His almighty hand,
   For clothes to wear
   And food to share,
For peace throughout the land.

Brenda Leigh

Photograph Opposite
CAVENDISH, VERMONT
John H. Vondell

Overleaf
Freelance Photographers Guild

Portrait of Autumn

The fog is lifting from the vales,
The air is fresh and clear.
In silhouette against the sky
The distant trees appear.

While in the east, the sleepy sun
Sends out its feeble rays
To stretch like giant tentacles
And blend in golden haze.

It touches every blade of grass
And every shrub and tree
And blends their yellow, red and green
In gorgeous harmony.

O Master Craftsman, would I knew
The secret of your art,
I'd paint its brilliant hues and tones
On every human heart.

Della Wade Peery

Autumn Patterns

The tang of evening autumn
penetrates the air,
the effervescent sunlight
is masked in smoky glare.
The wind slips through the treetops
at the close of day
and strips the colored trinkets
in aerial ballet.

Dusty-fingered cornstalks
rustling in the breeze,
singing tunes, forgotten,
with animated ease.
The rusty autumn colors
viewed through wisdom's eye,
like Oriental rugs, are sketched
in syncopated dye.

Prelude to the winter,
a mystical farewell,
a yearly memorandum
that summer cannot quell.
Nature weaves her patterns,
of this we can surmise,
prophetic fall will come again
in iridescent guise.

James Fly

Beyond Our Asking

More than hearts can imagine
  or minds comprehend,
God's bountiful gifts
  are ours without end.
We ask for a cupful
  when the vast sea is ours,
We pick a small rosebud
  from a garden of flowers,

We reach for a sunbeam
  but the sun still abides,
We draw one short breath
  but there's air on all sides.
Whatever we ask for
  falls short of God's giving

For his greatness exceeds
  every facet of living,
And always God's ready
  and eager and willing
To pour out his mercy
  completely fulfilling

All of man's needs
  for peace, joy and rest
For God gives his children
  Whatever is best.
Just give Him a chance
  to open his treasures
And He'll fill your life
  with unfathomable pleasures,

Pleasures that never
  grow worn out and faded
And leave us depleted,
  disillusioned and jaded.
For God has a "storehouse"
  just filled to the brim
With all that man needs
  if we'll only ask Him.

Helen Steiner Rice

Photograph Opposite
Fred Sieb

Mrs. Hale's
Original Thanksgiving Recipes

In 1621 the Pilgrims, in gratitude to God, sat down to a feast of thanksgiving. It was, however, 242 years later before this nation as a whole began a tradition based upon the Pilgrims' observance. That we have a national holiday of thanksgiving at all is due to an unceasing seventeen-year campaign of Sarah Josepha Hale.

The holiday of thanksgiving was not unknown to Americans when Mrs. Hale began her campaign; it was just not an organized affair. Various states set aside different days during the autumn as a time for giving thanks. In some states this day coincided with the closing of the canals so young boatmen could participate in the family gatherings; on Long Island, thanksgiving was always after the cows had been herded home from their meadows by the sea. Mrs. Hale, however, saw the advantages of six million people commemorating and giving thanks for the past year's accomplishments. She envisioned a national holiday corresponding to that of Independence Day.

In 1846, Mrs. Hale began her campaign to have the last Thursday of November declared Thanksgiving Day. She was, at the time, editor of *Godey's Lady's Book,* and it was from this platform that she began her campaign. Every autumn for seventeen years, readers of *Godey's* were assailed with editorials pointing out the advantages of a national holiday of Thanksgiving plus issues featuring foods of the harvest along with various ways of preparing them. Endeavoring to personally take her cause before the American people, Mrs. Hale also sent handwritten letters to thousands of people. Politicians, ministers and housewives received her epistles urging an official day of thanksgiving.

Finally, her efforts were rewarded. Some historians believe that Mrs. Hale personally visited President Lincoln; but in any event, on October 3, 1863, he issued a proclamation declaring a national holiday of Thanksgiving. In that address, Lincoln found much for which a war-torn nation could give thanks. He said, in part:

> It is a time peculiarly fitting to give thanks since in the midst of civil war, peace has been preserved with all nations, order has been maintained, the laws have been respected, and harmony has prevailed except in the field of military conflict.

Mrs. Hale, at the age of seventy-five, was victorious—and so was the nation. Thanksgiving Day has come to be a time when Americans, in war or peace, affluence or poverty, can join hands and hearts throughout the country and, as one people, thank God for his blessings.

Photograph Opposite
Gerald Koser

Tomato bouillon
Fried oysters
Roast turkey with veal and mushroom stuffing
Broiled parsnips
Pumpkin custard—Cranberry apple pie

ROAST TURKEY WITH VEAL AND MUSHROOM STUFFING

 1 10-to-12-pound turkey
 1 bay leaf
 ½ cup celery tops and leaves
 6 sprigs parsley
 1 tablespoon salt
 4 cups water
10 cups stale homemade bread crumbs
 ¼ pound mushrooms, finely chopped
 2 teaspoons powdered sage
 2 teaspoons thyme
 1 teaspoon summer savory
 ½ cup minced parsley
 ¾ teaspoon freshly ground pepper
 ¾ cup butter
 ½ cup minced shallots
 ½ pound lean, ground veal
    Chicken stock or broth
 4 tablespoons flour

1. Dry the turkey's cavity with paper towels. Tear out any clumps of fat and reserve.

2. Combine the neck, gizzard, heart, liver, turkey fat, bay leaf, celery tops, parsley sprigs, one teaspoon salt and the water in a saucepan and bring to a boil. Reduce the heat, partially cover and simmer for one hour.

3. Strain the liquid and reserve. Mince the gizzard, heart and liver and reserve for the gravy. Discard the neck, celery and herbs.

4. In a large bowl, combine the bread crumbs, chopped mushrooms, sage, thyme, summer savory, minced parsley, remaining two teaspoons salt and one-half teaspoon pepper. Toss until well blended.

5. Melt the butter in a large skillet. Add the minced shallots and cook for five minutes or until soft. Stir in the ground veal, breaking up any lumps, and sauté the mixture until the veal turns grayish white. Scrape the contents of the skillet onto the bread-crumb mixture and toss well. Adjust the seasonings.

6. Preheat oven to 450 degrees.

7. Stuff the turkey with the bread-crumb mixture, taking care not to overpack it. Sew the openings securely closed. Truss the bird. Rub remaining pepper into its skin.

8. Place the turkey, breast-side up, in the oven. Roast for 25 minutes, until skin is crisp and tanned. Lower the heat to 325 and pour one-half cup of the reserved turkey stock over the bird. Repeat twice, at 15-minute intervals, each time using one-half cup more of the turkey stock.

9. Continue to roast the bird for one and one-half hours longer, or about two and one-half hours altogether, basting at 15-minute intervals with the pan juices. To test if the turkey is completely cooked after this period, pierce the thigh with the tines of a fork. If the juices run clear, it is done. If they are pinkish, continue roasting for another 10 to 15 minutes. Transfer the turkey to a warmed platter.

10. Measure the remaining turkey stock. Add enough chicken stock to make three cups.

11. To make the gravy, skim off all but a thin film of fat from the juices left in the roasting pan. Stir in the flour. Cook over moderate heat, scraping up any particles left clinging to the pan. Pour in the stock and stir until the gravy comes to a boil and thickens. Taste for seasoning. Add the reserved turkey giblets and keep warm until ready to serve.

Yield: Eight to 10 servings.

FRIED OYSTERS

1½ pints shucked oysters (about 30 large ones)
 2 eggs
 1 tablespoon milk
 2 cups homemade bread crumbs
 2 teaspoons grated lemon rind
 1 teaspoon dried tarragon leaves, crushed in a mortar with a pestle
 2 teaspoons chopped chives
 1 tablespoon minced parsley
12 tablespoons clarified butter
    Salt and freshly ground pepper
    Lemon wedges

1. Pat the oysters dry with paper towels.

2. In a shallow bowl, beat the eggs with the milk.

3. Combine the bread crumbs, lemon rind, tarragon, chives and parsley in a bowl and stir until well blended. Spread the mixture out on two paper towels.

4. Heat the butter in a heavy skillet large enough to hold 10 oysters without crowding. When it is very hot, dip the oysters, one at a time, into the beaten egg mixture. Coat each oyster well with bread crumbs. Fry two to three minutes on each side or until oysters are brown and crisp. Drain on paper towels, remove to a hot platter and keep warm. Repeat the process until all the oysters have been fried.

5. Sprinkle with salt and pepper to taste. Serve with lemon wedges.

Yield: Ten servings.

CRANBERRY APPLE PIE

Pastry:
    9 tablespoons sweet butter
    3 tablespoons lard
 2¼ cups flour
    3 teaspoons sugar
  ¾ teaspoon salt
    4 to 5 tablespoons ice water
Filling:
    1 cup cranberries, about one-quarter pound
    4 large, tart apples, about one and one-half pounds
 1½ cups sugar
    1 tablespoon grated orange rind
    1 egg yolk
    1 teaspoon water

1. For the pastry, cut the butter and lard into small pieces and keep chilled until ready to use.

2. Combine the flour, sugar and salt together in a large mixing bowl. Add the chilled butter and lard bits. Cut the ingredients together with a pastry blender until the mixture resembles coarse meal.

3. Sprinkle four tablespoons of ice water over the mixture stirring with a fork to blend. Gather the dough into a ball. If the dough seems crumbly, add the remaining tablespoon of water.

4. Divide the dough into two parts, with one of the portions about one-third larger than the other. Flatten them with the palm of a hand. Wrap in wax paper and refrigerate for one hour.

5. Roll the larger portion into a circle about one-eighth-inch thick and 12 inches in diameter. Drape it over the rolling pin and transfer it to a nine-inch pie plate. Trim off any excess dough. Roll the remaining dough into a 10-inch round, cut slashes in the center and reserve.

6. Preheat oven to 450 degrees.

7. Coarsely chop the cranberries in a food processor or by hand.

8. Peel the apples and cut them into quarters. Remove the cores and slice.

9. Combine the cranberries, apples, sugar and orange rind in a large mixing bowl and toss until the sugar is completely distributed.

10. Transfer the mixture to the pie shell, mounding it high in the center. Moisten the edges of the shell with water. Place the reserved pastry round on top of the apple mixture, trim off any excess dough and crimp the rim.

11. Brush the surface of the pie with the egg yolk beaten with one teaspoon of water. Place the pie in the oven and bake for 10 minutes. Reduce the heat to 350 degrees and bake 50 to 60 minutes longer.

Yield: Eight servings.

TOMATO BOUILLON

 12 cups strong beef stock
    5 cups canned tomatoes with their juice
 10 whole peppercorns
 10 whole cloves
  ¼ cup chopped onion
    8 sprigs parsley
    1 teaspoon oregano
    6 egg whites
    6 egg shells, crushed
      Lemon slices

1. Skim off any fat floating on the surface of the beef stock.

2. In a large pot, combine the stock, tomatoes and their juice, peppercorns, cloves, chopped onion, parsley and oregano and bring to a boil. Reduce the heat and simmer 15 minutes. Set aside and allow to cool completely.

3. Lightly beat the egg whites until frothy. Add with the crushed egg shells to the beef-stock and tomato mixture. Bring to a boil, stirring constantly. Lower the heat and allow to simmer undisturbed for 20 minutes.

4. Gently ladle the bouillon through a sieve lined with a double thickness of cheesecloth into a large saucepan. Do not press down on the vegetables or the bouillon will be cloudy. Taste for seasoning.

5. Heat just before serving. Garnish with the lemon slices.

Yield: Ten servings.

BROILED PARSNIPS

    3 pounds parsnips
      Salt
    3 tablespoons lemon juice
    6 tablespoons melted butter
      Freshly ground pepper
    2 tablespoons butter, softened
  ¼ cup minced parsley

1. Peel the parsnips and trim off both ends. Cut into one-quarter-inch slices lengthwise.

2. Place in a pot of boiling salted water to cover and simmer over low heat until just tender, 10 to 15 minutes. Drain in a colander and allow to cool completely.

3. Generously butter a shallow baking dish large enough to hold the parsnips in one layer, and arrange them flat-side up, overlapping only slightly if necessary.

4. Sprinkle the parsnips with lemon juice, the melted butter and salt and pepper to taste, and place them in a preheated broiler, about eight inches from the flame, for five minutes. Bring the baking dish closer to the flame for the last minute to brown the parsnips slightly.

5. Dot with the softened butter, sprinkle with parsley and serve immediately.

Yield: Ten servings.

A Song for October

I could go out in the upper pasture and sit for an hour, and I would be in the very midst of the bounty, the beauty, the wholeness that makes the year complete without cutting it off from yesterday or tomorrow. All I would have to do would be to lift my face to the sky, that incredibly blue sky of a perfect October day, and open the pores of my understanding. The maples are like sunrise, and the oaks are like a stormy sky at dusk, and the ash trees that line the lower fencerow are almost as blue as the sky itself. The pasture grasses are still green, but the thistleheads are being ragged out into glistening clouds by the goldfinches. The squirrels have harvested the hickory nuts and the butternuts, leaving heaps of hulls as evidence of the plenty. The chipmunks have their granaries stocked and sit in the sun, even as I do, contemplating this marvelous world, this world of wealth in which to share. The crows proclaim their sovereignty, now that the flickers and kingbirds are gone, and the jays scream dissent at a distance. And overhead is, or soon will be, the gabble of geese.

I could stay, but the geese and my heart say go. Go and see the truth of October, know the enduring reality of this land that I love. So we probably shall go, if only so we can chant, eventually, with the old Navajo singers, "Beauty all around me, with it I return. Now on the trail of beauty, there I return."

Hal Borland

Photograph Opposite
Alpha Photo Associates

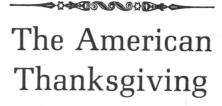

The American Thanksgiving

"Our harvest being gotten in, our governor sent four men on fowling, that we might after a special manner rejoice together after we had gathered the fruit of our labors. The four in one day killed as much fowl as, with a little help beside, served the company almost a week. At which time, amongst other recreations, we exercised our arms, many of the Indians coming amongst us, and among the rest their greatest king Massasoit, with some ninety men, whom for three days we entertained and feasted, and they went out and killed five deer, which they brought to the plantation and bestowed on our governor, and upon the captain and others. And although it be not always so plentiful as it was at this time with us, yet by the goodness of God, we are so far from want that we often wish you partakers of our plenty."

So wrote Pilgrim Edward Winslow to a friend in England shortly after the colonists of New Plymouth celebrated their first successful harvest. This brief passage is the only eyewitness description of the events that were to become the basis of a uniquely American holiday: Thanksgiving. As with so many of the facts of the Pilgrims' first years in America this occasion has become so imbued with tradition that it is difficult to place it in the perspective it occupied in Winslow's eyes. Indeed, any reference to giving thanks is notably missing from Winslow's description. What took place on that fall day some three-and-a-half centuries ago is best understood as the first recorded English harvest festival held on American soil, the acting out of an institution of great antiquity in the England the Pilgrims had left behind.

Harvest festivals combining prayers, sacrifices and rituals for the appropriate deity and joyful reveling at the accomplishment of a full granary and an end to the year's toil can be said to be old as harvests. The tiny farming community of Plymouth had special cause to celebrate in the autumn of 1621, for the people had established a firm foothold in their new home, as witness the successful crop of Indian corn that they had gathered.

In the winter months that immediately followed their landing at Plymouth in 1620, nearly half of the settlers had perished. Still, they had planted a crop in the spring. They had erected houses for shelter where there had been none. And they had won the trust, friendship and aid of the Indians. Now the harvest was proof of their ability to survive. And if they needed more precedent than centuries of tradition in their native land for the harvest celebration they held, there were references to harvest festivals in the Old Testament to which these avid students of the Scriptures could turn.

History does not record the reason for the decision—if it was in fact a decision rather than merely spontaneous reaction to circumstances—to hold a harvest festival rather than to proclaim a day of thanksgiving for that first New England harvest. Government-proclaimed days of thanksgiving, upon which everyone was to rest and offer prayers to God for some special providence, were well known to the Pilgrims. But the association of the day-of-thanksgiving-and-prayer concept with the fall harvest is something that happened subsequent to 1621 in New England.

There is no mention of Plymouth's celebrating the harvest in 1622, and perhaps it did not, for the yield was meager. In July of 1623, Governor William Bradford proclaimed the thirtieth of that month as a day of prayer and thanksgiving for the entire colony in gratitude for deliverance from a drought which had threatened yet another year of privation. In the years that followed, the individual towns and sometimes entire colonies of New England pro-

claimed days of thanksgiving at various times during the year on an independent basis, governed by whatever particular providences each felt obliged to acknowledge. There might be several in a single year for a given community. Most of the thanksgiving days one finds reference to in the surviving seventeenth-century colonial records are not related to the harvest. The occurrence of a fall day of thanksgiving associated with a harvest feast seems to have become general practice in the New England colonies and others by the time of the Revolutionary War, but the date of celebration varied according to local preference.

The first national day of Thanksgiving was Thursday, November 26, 1789. It was proclaimed by President Washington, not in response to the bounties of the harvest but in gratitude for the establishment of the Constitution of the United States. However, Thanksgiving did not become an annual national holiday following the Washington proclamation. Later presidents were indifferent or opposed to such proclamations, and there was a strong tradition for keeping the fall festivities responsive to local conditions.

The second National Thanksgiving Proclamation was issued by President Lincoln, in 1863, designating that the last Thursday in November would be set aside for the entire nation to give thanks together that despite the Civil War things were not so bad for the country as they might have been. The Lincoln proclamation was apparently in response to the efforts of Mrs. Sara Josepha Hale, editor of *Godey's Lady's Book*, who had been campaigning for the institution of a national Thanksgiving day since 1827.

Every president since Lincoln has continued the practice of proclaiming a day of Thanksgiving in the latter half of November. The local New England harvest-feast thanksgivings have given way to the national celebration, although the harvest has been "home" for some weeks by that time of year. Plimoth Plantation, in attempting to re-create for its visitors something of the life of the English people who settled here in the early seventeenth century has chosen to return to the earlier New England practice of celebrating the blessing of a good harvest at "harvest-time," in the best tradition of Plymouth's citizens of 1621.

Feast Time of the Year

This is the feast-time of the year,
When Plenty pours her wine of cheer,
And even humble boards may spare
To poorer poor a kindly share.
While bursting barns and granaries know
A richer, fuller overflow,
And they who dwell in golden ease
Bless without toil, yet toil to please.
This is the feast-time of the year,
The blessed advent draweth near;
Let rich and poor together break
The bread of love for Christ's sweet sake,
Against the time when rich and poor
Must ope for Him a common door,
Who comes a guest, yet makes a feast,
And bids the greatest and the least.

Dora Read Goodale

Hometown

In northeastern Illinois, just west of Chicago, where the plains are free to stretch from the congestion of the city and the woodlands grow undisturbed in a pattern of beauty and opulence, a friendly little village stands nestled in a bend of the Des Plaines River. "A village in a park," its proud inhabitants call it, an oasis in a desert of super highways and urban development. This is Riverside. It is where I live and where I grew up; where I, and generations before me, have laughed and cried and dreamed and loved.

Riverside is a warmhearted place. Its peaceful little roads curve gracefully between the groves of oaks and maples that shade the old homes. A crisp breeze gently brushes through the boughs of the trees, carrying off an occasional leaf and rocking the branches to and fro. The chirps and trills of the robins and bluejays are the only sounds that pervade the lazy tranquillity. Along the roadside, the milkman stops to make his delivery. The paperboy throws, invariably missing the porch step, and the morning paper lands in the bushes. These are common scenes and everyday happenings, yet are enchanting in their way. One can hardly mistake the bewitching sense of charm and affection that such trivial occurrences invite.

The atmosphere seems calculated to encourage a sentimental tear or two from those who have lived or grown up in Riverside. But to all of us, caught in the midst of a dubious present and a hazy and perplexing future, the past can sometimes become a dream remembered, a sanctuary for those who have grown a little older and a little wiser.

A boy, however, has no such past upon which to look, no experiences by which to gain wisdom or to guide his behavior; only age brings those treasures. He stands new, fresh and hopeful, at the beginning of life. Adventure lies before him with its miracles and wonders which only youth can recognize.

As I gaze out my window at the lofty trees and stately old buildings, with the sunlight beaming through the lace branches and leaves, my mind invariably turns to thoughts of the past. How often I, as a boy, walked along those byways and played among the trees or stood and watched the river flow beneath the bridge and the birds fly south. Every forest, every hill and street and gaslight is filled with fond memories. I remember Riverside; it is here that breathes the spirit of my boyhood.

I sigh and gently recline in my chair. My eyes grow heavy with the intoxicating thoughts, and for a moment I see my hometown through the eyes of a child. Again I feel the tingle of a breeze whiffing past my ears, and I remember walks down peaceful streets, warm regards of friendly neighbors, the soda fountain at the corner drugstore, the old swinging bridge. I see the significance of those familiar places and faces, significance which comes to me only now in reflection. For a moment I look upon my hometown and recognize the magic which has ever given me sustenance, and which has been the essence of all hometowns.

I cannot help but see my village through different eyes. No longer the dazzled eyes of youth, they are, instead, the eyes of wisdom. They see Riverside not only as a private world, but as a member of the union of countless hometowns across the country, as a part of that magnificent American undertaking. Indeed, the old houses, the parkways, the curving roads appear the same, yet something more endures. As the spirit of my childhood lives here, so the essence of courage, faith and strength breathes like a whisper in the wind. To be sure, the soul of our country rests within ten thousand home-

towns such as this. Assurance gained from a simple life and compassion gained from our convictions steady us in life. Here my village stands as a monument from the past, of the present and for the future.

I shake the dreams from my eyes and gaze out the window again. Evening has come to Riverside; the gaslights are aglow, the moon and stars shine in their places, and the distant sound of a passing train echoes softly through the night. Most of my neighbors are at home now and their children tucked in bed. Only a few lights remain to dot the darkness.

Tomorrow will bring a new day to my hometown, and people will rise and go about their business as they have done with every dawn for countless years. There will be laughter, of course, some tears, happiness, a look toward the future. And there will be growth. No monumental world decisions will be made here, no climactic world crisis solved. Rather, human beings will experience the simple events of life among their families and with their friends. They will know for another day the pride of belonging and the warmth of their interdependence. It will be an ordinary day.

John Slobodnik

I Yield Thee Praise

For thoughts that curve like winging birds
Out of the summer dusk each time
I drink the splendor of the sky
And touch the wood-winds swinging by—
    I yield Thee praise.

For waves that lift from autumn seas
To spill strange music on the land,
The broken nocturne of a lark
Flung out upon the lonely dark—
    I yield Thee praise.

For rain that piles gray torrents down
Black mountain gullies to the plain,
For singing fields and crimson flare
At daybreak, and the sea-sweet air—
    I yield Thee praise.

For gentle mists that wander in
To hide the tired world outside
That in our hearts old lips may smile
Their blessing through life's afterwhile—
    I yield Thee praise.

For hopes that fight like stubborn grass
Up through the clinging snows of fear
To find the rich earth richer still
With kindliness and honest will—
    I yield Thee praise.

Philip Jerome Cleveland

Photograph Opposite
Freelance Photographers Guild

Hiawatha's Childhood

By the shores of Gitche Gumee,
By the shining Big-Sea-Water,
Stood the wigwam of Nokomis,
Daughter of the Moon, Nokomis.
Dark behind it rose the forest,
Rose the black and gloomy pine-trees,
Rose the firs with cones upon them;
Bright before it beat the water,
Beat the clear and sunny water,
Beat the shining Big-Sea-Water.

There the wrinkled old Nokomis
Nursed the little Hiawatha,
Rocked him in his linden cradle,
Bedded soft in moss and rushes,
Safely bound with reindeer sinews;
Stilled his fretful wail by saying,
"Hush! the Naked Bear will hear thee!"
Lulled him into slumber, singing,
"Ewa-yea! my little owlet!
Who is this, that lights the wigwam?
With his great eyes lights the wigwam?
Ewa-yea! my little owlet!"

Many things Nokomis taught him
Of the stars that shine in heaven;
Showed him Ishkoodah, the comet,
Ishkoodah, with fiery tresses;
Showed the Death-Dance of the spirits,
Warriors with their plumes and war-clubs,
Flaring far away to northward
In the frosty nights of winter;
Showed the broad white road in heaven,
Pathway of the ghosts, the shadows,
Running straight across the heavens,
Crowded with the ghosts, the shadows.

At the door on summer evenings,
Sat the little Hiawatha;
Heard the whispering of the pine-trees,
Heard the lapping of the waters,
Sounds of music, words of wonder;
"Minne-wawa!" said the pine-trees,
"Mudway-aushka!" said the water.

Saw the fire-fly Wah-wah-taysee,
Flitting through the dusk of evening,
With the twinkle of its candle
Lighting up the brakes and bushes,
And he sang the song of children,
Sang the song Nokomis taught him.

"Wah-wah-taysee, little fire-fly,
Little, flitting, white-fire insect,
Little, dancing, white-fire creature,
Light me with your little candle,
Ere upon my bed I lay me,
Ere in sleep I close my eyelids!"

Saw the moon rise from the water,
Rippling, rounding from the water,
Saw the flecks and shadows on it,
Whispered, "What is that, Nokomis?"
And the good Nokomis answered:
"Once a warrior, very angry,
Seized his grandmother and threw her

Up into the sky at midnight;
Right against the moon he threw her;
'Tis her body that you see there."

Saw the rainbow in the heaven,
In the eastern sky the rainbow,
Whispered, "What is that, Nokomis?"
And the good Nokomis answered:
" 'Tis the heaven of flowers you see there;
All the wild-flowers of the forest,
All the lilies of the prairie,
When on earth they fade and perish,
Blossom in that heaven above us."

When he heard the owls at midnight,
Hooting, laughing in the forest,
"What is that?" he cried in terror;
"What is that," he said, "Nokomis?"
And the good Nokomis answered:
"That is but the owl and owlet,
Talking in their native language,
Talking, scolding at each other."

Then the little Hiawatha
Learned of every bird its language,
Learned their names and all their secrets,
How they built their nests in summer,
Where they hid themselves in winter,
Talked with them whene'er he met them,
Called them "Hiawatha's Chickens."

Of all beasts he learned the language,
Learned their names and all their secrets,
How the beavers built their lodges,
Where the squirrels hid their acorns,
How the reindeer ran so swiftly,
Why the rabbit was so timid,
Talked with them whene'er he met them,
Called them "Hiawatha's Brothers."

Henry Wadsworth Longfellow

Stand
with Me Here

Stand with me here
Where the sun's long streamers
Float like ribbons in the wind,
Memories upon the mind's cool breeze.
I seem a piece of driftwood washed here
By a stream that changed its course long ago—
Exiled by chance.
Here still the autumn lingers
With the evening.
The sun sprays its last bit of yellow liquid
On prairie grass almost too blond for grazing;
And, on a field of stubble farther to the west,
The tiny shafts of gold
Reach up to drink the dew.

Feel with me here
This friendliness that comes of listening
To the creek's low whisper
Just before freezing,
To the slow metallic clang of cowbells
Calling louder and closer
At the hour when daylight swings
On the flaxen ropes of evening.

Stay with me here
Where heifers tarry along the path—
Where thyme and pennyroyal are autumn-curled,
And sumac bobs are wakened embers on a
    hearth—
And milkweed pods burst in silver, newborn
    stars.
For a moment I start, remembering—
It seems but yesterday—
I filled my apron pocket with sticky furry pods.
It was the autumn grandmother made fluff-ball
    tiebacks
For the lace curtains
That hung at the parlor windows—

For each tieback three balls were tinted purple
With elderberry ink
And two, the color of a summer sky
With blueing from the wash-house cupboard.
But one she left as from the field,
Wind blown and flossy white.
She tied them with a cord
As yellow as the brass of curtain rings,
Bright as the flutted knobs
At the ends of the poles
Then let them hang unevenly below the sill—
A blue one, like a fallen star, cooled,
Touched the maple leaf design
Where the ingrain carpet met the wall.
Walk with me here
Where the wild flakes will swirl
Tomorrow
Or the day after—
Where ice will sharpen to swords
The gaunt branches of wild shrubs
And heifers will lie in cud-chewing drowsiness
On a straw-warm stable floor.

Stand with me here
For it is now that I know
And it is here that I feel
That thoughts breathe and live and have their
    being
In memories of unforgettable taste
As tang from cider flagons,
In unforgettable sound
As slow water over pebbles,
In unforgettable silence
Like sun on stubble—
And even though I do not live here
And may not walk here each day
As my forebears did,
Stand with me now,
Hand answering hand,
That I may keep this visit's memory
A covenant with peace that only pastures know—
Holy in the late sunlight.

And she who tied them must have felt
This sacred silence
That spreads like dew on stubble
Or sunfall over pasture.

Ethel Green Russell

'Twas the week of Thanksgiving
    In old Plymouth town,
The housecleaning over,
    The crops bedded down,
When townsfolk decided
    This great harvest hoard
Be shared with others,
    In praise of the Lord.
A runner was chosen
    Who hurried away
To invite the Indians
    To a thanks-giving day.
They began preparations
    As soon as the sun
Came up the next morning;
    There was much to be done.
Monday was scheduled
    For washing the clothes,

'Twas the Week

Sorting and mending
    And drying in rows.
On Tuesday the women
    Were baking supplies:
Apple, gooseberry,
    And dark mincemeat pies.
That old kitchen fragrance
    In so many ways
Was a special reminder
    Of their sweet childhood days.
When cool, pies were sorted
    And placed upon shelves
So high up that children
    Could not help themselves.
The baking continued
    On Wednesday, and then
There were puddings, fruitcakes,
    And pound cakes in tin.

# of Thanksgiving

Wild turkeys for cleaning,
  Enough for a week
With panfish and seafood
  From Bay shore and creek.
Indians sent venison
  Which the men helped prepare;
They added some wild geese
  With popcorn to share.
Then on Thursday morning
  When the fire coals were hot,
The meat turned on spits,
  Stews simmered in pots.
Lobster and oysters
  Roasted over hot coals
And Indian pudding
  Baked in heavy crock bowls.
Biscuits and hoecakes,
  Butter, fresh churned,

When this festive array
  Was done "to a turn,"
The Governor spoke
  In his most reverent way;
He asked for God's blessing
  On Thanksgiving Day!
It must have been grand
  And fun, so to speak,
The celebration lasted
  The rest of the week.
Then Pilgrims of Plymouth
  And Indians, too,
Were changed ever after;
  The feeling was new.
They broke bread together;
  Shared grateful amens,
They met as rank strangers,
  They parted good friends.

Alice Leedy Mason

Because of Thy Great Bounty

Because I have been given much,
I, too, shall give;
Because of Thy great bounty, Lord,
Each day I live
I shall divide my gifts from Thee
With every brother that I see
Who has the need of help from me.

Because I have been sheltered, fed,
By Thy good care,
I cannot see another's lack
And I not share
My glowing fire, my loaf of bread,
My roof's safe shelter overhead,
That he, too, may be comforted.

Because love has been lavished so
Upon me, Lord,
A wealth I know that was not meant
For me to hoard,
I shall give love to those in need,
The cold and hungry clothe and feed,
Thus shall I show my thanks indeed.

Grace Noll Crowell

*Photograph Opposite
Robert Cushman Hayes*

Thanksgiving as an Expression of the American Spirit

This oldest festival,
   dating from the heroic age of America,
   is the best expression of our national spirit.

It combines into one conception
   productive enterprise,
   domestic felicity,
   and religious devotion.

Thanksgiving Day represents the fruits of industry
   turned to family festivity and sanctified by prayer.

It was instituted by men of culture
   and women of refinement
   who showed themselves willing to suffer
   persecution, imprisonment, banishment
   from the comforts of an English home,
   exile across the sea, cold, hunger, pestilence,
   and death for their principles.

Those principles are today the richest treasure
   and the brightest hope for humanity.

They are the stuff of which heroes were made
   and by which a nation was nurtured to its manhood.

These three principles
   are the legacy which that heroic age
   has bequeathed to us, its heirs:
   self-government in the state,
   freedom for the Church, goodwill toward mankind.

Let us cherish these principles,
   for in them lie the essence, the beauty,
   the strength of American institutions,
   and the warrant of their perpetuity.

Adapted from Joseph Parrish Thompson

First Snow on the Farm

Our summer days so quickly fled;
The autumn leaves have played their song
And now it's wintertime instead,
With days so short and nights so long.
Our birds have flown to warmer site,
The leafless trees in dreamland sleep,
The snow lies deep, so soft and white,
And watchful stars their vigil keep.

Big barns are crammed with grain and hay;
Our cellars packed with things to eat,
"Contented cows" in feedlots stay,
Corrals are full of woolly sheep.
Young folks and old swarm through the hills,
With snowmobiles and skis and skates,
For days of fun, with thrills and spills,
Cold winter makes just what it takes.

For some who care for ease and rest
And those unfit for rugged play,
A well-warmed house makes cozy nest
To while away the winter's stay.
The Lord be thanked for seasons four,
Each crowned with glory all its own,
In mountains high, near Heaven's door,
Where home is truly "Home Sweet Home."

A. G. Seaver

Over the River and through the Woods

Over the river, and through the wood,
To grandfather's house we go;
The horse knows the way,
To carry the sleigh,
Through the white and drifted snow.

Over the river, and through the wood—
Oh, how the wind does blow!
It stings the toes,
And bites the nose
As over the ground we go.

Over the river, and through the wood,
  To have a first-rate play.
    Hear the bells ring,
    "Ting-a-ling-ding!"
  Hurrah for Thanksgiving Day!

Over the river and through the wood
  Trot fast, my dapple-gray!
    Spring over the ground
    Like a hunting-hound!
  For this is Thanksgiving Day.

Over the river and through the wood,
  And straight through the barn-yard gate.
    We seem to go
    Extremely slow,
  It is so hard to wait!

Over the river and through the wood—
  Now grandmother's cap I spy!
    Hurrah for the fun!
    Is the pudding done?
  Hurrah for the pumpkin pie!

Lydia Maria Child

Ideals' Pages
from the Past

On the following six pages
we are presenting a selection
from Homespun Ideals 1954.

Where Old Roads Wind

Agnes Davenport Bond

Through leafy underbrush an old road leads,
Now overgrown with vagrant grass and weeds.
High centers rise between the well-worn tracks,
Where many wheels upheld their heavy packs,
Where horses, one time, pranced or trod along —
Roads now untraveled by the hurried throng.

Those were the days when simple joys brought thrills,
Like trails that led into the distant hills,
Where curving roadways turned to cottage lights
That glowed with welcome on the winter nights,
Where friendliness was ample to outweigh
The rush and hustle of the present day.

Is something lost one cannot know again?
That peaceful living in the lives of men.

THANKSGIVING

Edgar Daniel Kramer

Dear Lord, for the winds of winter,
   That danced with the drifting snows;
For the silver rains of April,
   And Junetime's flaming rose
That thrilled to the sun's hot kisses
   And hearkened the honey bees
Humming away to pillage
   The sweets of the clover leas;

For the dew that gleamed on the grasses;
   For the dawn that smiled from the hill
When we rode from the barn to the plowing
   Through a world that was strangely still,
Except for the tinkling of trace chains
   And the clumping of horses' feet
That lifted a startled skylark
   With singing up from the wheat;

For the creaking of harness leathers;
   For the whisper of new-turned sod
And the clucking of hens that feasted
   On grubs from the crumbling clod,
While we toiled through the fleeting hours,
   Until the brief day was through,
Keeping our plowshares steady
   And laying our furrows true;

For the strength and the will to labor
   With the mattock and hoe and bar;
For the weariness born of toiling
   And the peace that came from afar,
When all of the chores were finished
   And we turned to the lamp-light's gleam,
That beckoned to us from the kitchen
   And called us to rest and dream —
   — We give Thee thanks!

Dear Lord, for the earth's rich largess,
   That our hands have gathered in
And stored where the silent shadows
   Are guarding each mow and bin:

The fruits of the mystic sowing,
   The harvesting's golden yield
That we have gladly garnered
   From orchard and wood and field;
For apples and fragrant honey,
   For shellbarks and corn and wheat,
For grapes that were purple fire
   In a dusk that was strangely sweet;

For yellow, moon-faced pumpkins,
   That lay on the age-old earth
And leaned to the squirrels' chatter,
   That echoed the rabbits' mirth;
For neighbors who know our failings
   And yet are our steadfast friends;
For loved ones who wait our coming,
   When the toiling of each day ends,
And, flinging the door wide open
   At the sound of our weary tread,
Lead us with clinging kisses
   To our hard-earned meat and bread;

For shelter from wind and weather;
   For a seat in the chimney nook,
Where we dream and smoke by the fire
   Or browse through a much-thumbed book;
For love that is balm for anguish;
   For hope that is flouting gloom;
For faith that is mocking winter
   With visions of lilac bloom —
   We give Thee thanks!

The Painting of the Leaves

Emilie A. Watson

The elves all grabbed a paint brush,
  and the paints of different hues;
They donned their smocks, and ran and got
  whatever they could use.
Then they shinnied up the tree trunks,
  and scattered on the limbs,
For Autumn winds had come once more,
  and the trees they had to trim.

Around the edges of the leaves,
  the first little elf trimmed red,
But the next one decided that he was wrong,
  and painted it yellow, instead.
Another one put a stroke of orange,
  and another, a stroke of brown,
And from all the weight of the little elves,
  the leaf came tumbling down.
But the elves continued painting,
  until every leaf was bright.
They started in the morning,
  and they painted thru the night.

And when, on the following morning,
  the sun came over the hill,
People came out of their houses, and their
  lungs just seemed to fill
With the wonderful air of Autumn, and they
  looked at the painted trees
That were reaching their arms to heaven
  and stirring in the breeze.
The people thought not of the labor —
  the hard work of the wee elves.
But they, the little fellows,
  were mighty proud of themselves!

Nature's Beauty

How beautiful the woodlands are
As autumn days unfold,
When maple leaves have turned to red
And poplars, brightest gold.

When stately firs and lofty pines
Are standing proud and green,
There is no beauty to compare
When nature paints a scene.

How lovely just to wander down
A shaded, leafy trail,
To pause beside a little brook
Where colored leaf-boats sail,

To watch them gently drift along
To some secluded pool
Where each one is reflected
In the water, clear and cool.

Though nature's beauty may surround us,
It's unseen by troubled eyes.
With the daily care of living,
Without thought, we pass it by.

But to those who are discerning,
Nature's beauties never cease;
And in its solitude, they find
Quiet strength and sweetest peace.

Naomi I. Parks

Coming in Christmas Ideals

An inspiring message by Pat Boone entitled "The Real Christmas" . . . a special feature on Christmas dinners as they were in Charles Dickens' time . . . a charming piece by noted speaker Paul Harvey on how Clement C. Moore's famous poem " 'Twas the Night Before Christmas" came into being . . . Best-Loved Poet Vera Hardman . . . Pages from the Past, Christmas Ideals 1953 . . . a new series of inspiring religious paintings . . . plus poetry, prose, artwork and photographs conveying the warmth and joy of the blessed Yuletide season.

ACKNOWLEDGMENTS

DISCOVERERS by Isabel Fiske Conant. From COLUMBUS DAY, Copyright 1938 by Hilah Paulmier and Robert Haven Schauffler. LORD, BLESS THIS HOUSE by James Dillet Freeman. Originally published by Unity School of Christianity. Used with permission. BEYOND OUR ASKING by Helen Steiner Rice. Used with permission of the author. THE DANCE OF THE LEAVES by Isla Paschal Richardson. From MY BED-TIME GAME by Isla Paschal Richardson. Copyright 1949 by Isla Paschal Richardson. Used with permission. LITTLE ORPHANT ANNIE by James Whitcomb Riley. From JOYFUL POEMS FOR CHILDREN by James Whitcomb Riley, copyright © 1941, 1946 and 1960 by Lesley Payne, Elizabeth Miesse and Edmund H. Eitel. Reprinted by permission of the publisher, the Bobbs-Merrill Company, Inc. SEPTEMBER by Garnett Ann Schultz. From SOMETHING BEAUTIFUL by Garnett Ann Schultz. Copyright © 1966 by Garnett Ann Schultz. Published by Dorrance & Company. ON A PORTRAIT OF COLUMBUS by George S. Woodberry. From the Century Magazine. By permission of D. Appleton-Century Company, New York and Mr. Charles D. Woodberry. Recipes: Tomato Bouillon, Fried Oysters, Roast Turkey with Veal and Mushroom Stuffing, Pumpkin Custard, Cranberry Apple Pie and Broiled Parsnips. © 1976 by The New York Times Company. Reprinted by permission. Our sincere thanks to the following authors whose addresses we were unable to locate: Philip Jerome Cleveland for I YIELD THEE PRAISE; THE DIGNITY OF LABOR by Unknown Author, and THANKSGIVING AS AN EXPRESSION OF THE AMERICAN SPIRIT, adapted from Joseph Parrish Thompson. From THE FAITH OF AMERICA, compiled by Mordecai M. Kaplan, J. Paul Williams and Eugene Kohn. Copyright 1951.

Additional Photo Credits: Front cover, Gerald Koser. Inside front cover, Topsham, Vt., Fred Sieb. Inside back cover, Joseph Barnett. Back cover, Gerald Koser.

We just couldn't wait until Christmas . . .

to tell you about CHRISTMAS IDEALS!
And, if you're like most people, you can't wait either!

WE JUST COULDN'T WAIT! Christmas is so exciting . . . the color and cheer, the love and warmth . . . and CHRISTMAS IDEALS is our most colorful and exciting issue of the year. NO, WE COULDN'T WAIT to tell you and all your friends about the beautiful color photography and artwork that fills this issue from cover to cover, the warm and meaningful stories and the tender poetry that makes each page a celebration in itself. Visit breathtaking vistas from America's winter wonderland . . . the towering mountaintops and the still, quiet meadows. You, as well as all those fortunate enough to receive your gift of IDEALS, will experience the spiritual inspiration of an all new series of nativity paintings created especially for this beautiful issue. Share the true meaning of Christmas with one of America's favorite song stars, Pat Boone, in an enchanting story entitled, "The Real Christmas." Accompany noted radio personality, Paul Harvey, as he discovers how Clement C. Moore's famous story "The Night Before Christmas" actually came into being. Walk the hills around Bethlehem with Nathaniel Olson, an Ideals favorite, as he relates his feelings on first visiting the Holy Land.

NOW YOU SEE WHY WE JUST COULDN'T WAIT! CHRISTMAS IDEALS is one Christmas gift we HAD to tell you about! So, now that you know, you owe it to yourself and your friends to discover WHY we are so excited. Subscribe to IDEALS today! Find out for yourself why CHRISTMAS IDEALS has become an American Christmas tradition.

Discover also how you can realize substantial savings by subscribing NOW! As of November 1, 1978, the price for a single issue of IDEALS will increase from $2.50 to $2.75 and the cost of a one year subscription will increase from $10.00 to $12.00. By SUBSCRIBING NOW you will save $2.00 under the cost of the new subscription rates. Don't miss this opportunity to subscribe now at the old subscription rates. THIS OFFER CAN NOT BE REPEATED!

So, act now! Enter your subscription today. And, now that the secret is out, why not tell all your friends! Better yet, why not surprise them this Christmas with a gift subscription to IDEALS! You needn't send any money now unless you prefer. Simply mark the proper area on the enclosed order blank and we'll bill you later.

IDEALS Single Issues $2.50

IDEALS SUBSCRIPTION PLANS

ONE YEAR . . . 6 issues as published $10.00
(Savings Value of $5.00 under the single copy rate.)

First Subscription	1-4 Additional	5 or More Additional
$10.00	$9.00 Each	$8.50 Each

TWO YEAR . . . 12 issues as published $17.00
(Savings Value of $13.00 under the single copy rate.)

First Subscription	1-4 Additional	5 or More Additional
$17.00	$15.00 Each	$14.50 Each

CHRISTMAS GIVING BEGINS WITH IDEALS

When you wish to express the fullness of your love, give the QUALITY GIFTBOOK . . . GIVE IDEALS!

HAVE A GOURMET CHRISTMAS is a sparkling new cookbook by the authors of the best-selling cookbook, *Gourmet on The Go,* Naomi Arbit and June Turner. An abundance of delicious gourmet recipes seasoned with a dash of holiday flare certain to compliment your holiday table. 03-00613—64 pages, soft cover, 2.50

IDEALS CHRISTMAS COOKBOOK has delighted holiday cooks for several years now and, due to popular demand, is back for another encore Christmas season. Packed with dozens of tempting holiday recipes, from delicious mealtime menus to exciting desserts, this is one cookbook you won't want to miss!

03-00602—64 pages, soft cover, 2.50

FAVORITE CHRISTMAS CAROLS FROM IDEALS is a melodious collection of your favorite Christmas carols just in time for this Christmas season. Whether your family enjoys singing around the piano or caroling door to door, this book will help you celebrate the season in the spirit of song for years to come. Church groups will also find this book the ideal caroling companion. So, order a good supply to meet your group's needs. 04-00474—32 pages, soft cover, 1.50

LET'S CELEBRATE CHRISTMAS proved to be one of our most popular releases last Christmas. And so, in time for this Christmas, we completely redesigned this popular book making it even more colorful and facinating than before. Read how Christmas is celebrated across America, from Bethlehem, Pennsylvania to San Francisco. It's a journey you won't forget!

04-00289—80 pages, soft cover, 3.95

THE CHRISTMAS MIRACLE is Ideals's all-new religious book for the holiday season. A rich treasury of essays written by the noted author and minister J. Harold Gwynne. Tucked among the prose are classical Christian poems by such revered authors as G. K. Chesterton, Phillis McGinley and Boris Pasternak. Featuring masterpieces by Leonardo da Vinci, Rembrandt and Murillo. 04-00046—80 pages, soft cover, 3.95

CHRISTMAS IS REMEMBERING is a colorful, nostalgic journey into Christmas past. Relive the enchantment of Christmas celebrations, all the warmth and cheer, that your grandparents enjoyed so much. Feel the thrill of slipping over the snow in a shiny new cutter or lighting the first candle on the family Christmas tree. Here are memories too vivid to forget!

04-00469—32 pages, soft cover, 2.25

DECORATING FOR THE HOLIDAYS poses the question, "How do you make Christmas decorating a new and innovating experience?" The answer? By using pine cones, fruits, holly sprigs and, most importantly, your own imagination. Author, Harold Cook, gives you detailed instructions on a wide variety of exciting Christmas wreaths, swags and floral arrangements—easy to make and beautiful to behold.

04-00286—64 pages, soft cover, 2.95

Brighten a child's Christmas this year

ONCE UPON A RHYME brings together all of the world's most beloved nursery rhymes and strikingly beautiful artwork to create a nursery rhyme book your children will cherish. From *Humpty Dumpty* to *Wee Willie Winkie,* all of your children's favorite nursery rhymes are included, each illustrated in fanciful artwork sure to make their eyes pop with each turn of the page.   04-00055—80 pages, soft cover, 3.95

JOLLY OLD SANTA CLAUS features George Hinke's famous series of brilliantly colored Santa Claus art masterpieces accompanied by a charming children's story about how Santa Claus and his elves prepare for Christmas Eve at the North Pole. Visit the North Pole and see the busy preparations in process and meet Mrs. Claus and all the reindeer too!   04-00448—40 pages, soft cover, 2.25

CHRISTMAS FOR CHILDREN is a child's poetry journey into the true spirit and meaning of Christmas. Christmas through a child's eyes is a fanciful experience and the brightly colored pictures in this book take you to this land of fancy and wonderment. Poems and stories from renowned children's authors are highlighted by the artwork of such famous children's painters as Miki and Francis Hook.   04-00450—32 pages, soft cover, 2.25

A CHRISTMAS CAROL, Charles Dickens' timeless tale of love and togetherness at Christmastime, springs to life in living color in the pages of this favorite Ideals' children's book. Illustrated by Charles Ropp and printed in an easy to read format, here is one Dickens' tale well worth rereading Christmas after Christmas!   04-00262—48 pages, soft cover, 2.95

THE NIGHT BEFORE CHRISTMAS is Ideals ALL COLOR rendition of Clement C. Moore's famous children's poem. Remember when you first heard this beautiful children's story and images of Christmas reindeer and "Old Saint Nick" filled your bedtime dreams? Why not give your little dreamers this charming Christmas tale to tuck under their pillows this Christmas!   04-00498—24 pages, soft cover, 1.95

NEW GIFT BOOKLETS

Are you looking for a holiday greeting that's, well . . . a little more than just a greeting card? Something that conveys everything you want to say? Something with lavish color pictures inside not just on the cover? Something that looks and feels expensive yet sells for a reasonable price? Well, look no more! Ideals has just what you need . . . the Ideals GIFT BOOKLET. Each Ideals GIFT BOOKLET looks and feels expensive with a handsome, full color laminated cover and 20 pages of holiday wishes and full color pictures inside! All of this for the low price of only $1.00. Why not give Ideals GIFT BOOKLETS this holiday season instead of greeting cards. You get more for your money . . . more of the thought you wish to express! Softcover—5⅜" x 7¼"—20 Pages—$1.00 Each.

AT LONG LAST! THE DELUXE CHRISTMAS BOOK IDEALS READERS HAVE BEEN ASKING FOR

IDEALS CHRISTMAS TREASURY

- 160 Pages
- 9" x 12"
- Full Color Dust Jacket
- Durable Hard Cover
- The Finest Enamel Stock
- Artwork of the Masters
- Over 50 Color Photographs and Illustrations
- Dozens of Charming Stories and Poems

AT LAST! Ideals has finally collected the finest of its volumes of Christmas photographs, artwork, poetry and prose and tastefully combined it together under one stunning color cover in a deluxe Christmas hard bound so startling in beauty, warmth and inspiration that only a 160 page, 9 x 12 book could contain it all! IDEALS CHRISTMAS TREASURY says Christmas in a BIG way at a price that is hard to beat. With page after page of the finest color reproductions as only Ideals can present them, this deluxe Christmas hard bound is a treasure chest of rich, brilliant color featuring some of the finest photography and artwork anywhere. Coupled with the traditional prose and poetry America has taken to its heart Christmas after Christmas, this book promises to be a collector's item in years to come.

Here are some of the exciting chapters you will enjoy:

- Holiday Preparations
- Winter Wonderland
- The Warmth Of Home At Christmas
- Christmas Through a Child's Eyes
- An Old Fashioned Christmas
- The Miracle of The Birth of Christ
- The Spirit of Giving
- Celebration of Song
- Christmas In Many Lands

With such featured authors as Charles Dickens, Hans Christian Anderson, Washington Irving and O. Henry . . . poets the likes of Eugene Field and Clement C. Moore . . . and such distinguished artists as Thomas Nast, George Hinke, Currier & Ives, Ludwig Kraus, G. H. Durie, A. Van Dyck and Peter Paul Rubens, IDEALS CHRISTMAS TREASURY is an unforgettable reading experience your entire family will enjoy.

04-00006—160 pages, hard cover, 9.95

My Personal Order

POSTAGE*		
USA	1. ORDERS UNDER $5.00 ADD	$ .75
	2. SUBSCRIPTIONS	NO CHARGE
	3. ALL GIFT BOOKS ADD	$ .10 per gift name
OUTSIDE USA	1. ORDERS UNDER $5.00 ADD	$1.00
	2. SUBSCRIPTIONS ADD	$1.00 per sub. year
	3. ALL GIFT BOOKS ADD	$ .15 per gift name

YOUR NAME

ADDRESS

CITY (   )

STATE   ZIP CODE

☐ master charge ☐ Charge my Master Charge   ☐ VISA ☐ Charge my BankAmericard/VISA   Exp. Date

Acct. No.

SIGNATURE

☐ IS THIS A NEW ADDRESS? ENTER ON BACK

PHONE (   )

IDEALS PERSONAL ACCOUNT NUMBER   FROM ADDRESS LABEL

ORDER TOLL FREE
800-558-4343
WISCONSIN-CANADA CALL COLLECT—414-771-2700
MINIMUM PHONE ORDER $10.00

MY IDEALS SUBSCRIPTION PLAN (FOR GIFT SUBSCRIPTIONS SEE OTHER SIDE)

1 YEAR SUBSCRIPTION $10.00	2 YEAR SUBSCRIPTION $17.00	3 YEAR SUBSCRIPTION $24.00
1-4 additional gift subs $9.00, or a total of 5 or more additional subs $8.50 ea.	1-4 additional gift subs $15.00, or a total of 5 or more additional gift subs $14.50 ea.	1-4 additional gift subs $21.50, or a total of 5 or more additional gift subs $20.50 ea.

BEAUTIFUL IDEALS ISSUES 8½ x 11 (SOFT COVER)

BK CODE	TITLE	PRICE	QTY	BK CODE	TITLE	PRICE	QTY
01-00318	FRIENDSHIP 12/78	2.75		01-00309	WOODLAND	2.50	
01-00317	CHRISTMAS	2.75		01-00308	HAPPINESS	2.50	
01-00316	THANKSGIVING	2.50		01-00305	INSPIRATION	2.50	
01-00315	COUNTRYSIDE	2.50		01-00303	MEMORY	2.50	
01-00314	NEIGHBORLY	2.50		01-00302	ADVENTURE	2.50	
01-00312	FIRESIDE	2.50		06-00713	IDEALS BINDER	4.50	

IDEALS COOKBOOKS 8½ x 11 (SOFT COVER)

BK CODE	TITLE	PRICE	QTY	BK CODE	TITLE	PRICE	QTY
03-00607	MAMA'S HONEY COOKBOOK	2.50		03-00633	COUNTRY KITCHEN COOKBOOK	2.50	
03-00610	THE GOURMET TOUCH	2.50		03-00634	AMERICAN COOKBOOK	2.50	
03-00658	GUIDE TO MICROWAVE COOKING	2.50		03-00628	IDEALS FAMILY COOKBOOK 1	2.50	
03-00613	HAVE A GOURMET CHRISTMAS	2.50		03-00640	OUTDOOR COOKBOOK	2.25	
03-00614	FAMILY FAVORITES FROM IDEALS	2.50		03-00604	SOUPS FOR ALL SEASONS	2.50	
03-00612	NICE AND EASY DESSERTS	2.50		03-00631	GOURMET ON THE GO	2.50	
03-00608	COUNTRY BREAD COOKBOOK 10/78	2.50		03-00637	MENUS FROM AROUND THE WORLD	2.50	
03-00602	IDEALS CHRISTMAS COOKBOOK	2.50		03-00606	TEMPTING TREASURES	2.50	
03-00639	IDEALS COOKIE COOKBOOK	2.50		03-00601	FESTIVE PARTY COOKBOOK	2.50	
03-00635	CHRISTMAS GIFTS FROM THE KITCH.	2.50		03-00636	SIMPLY DELICIOUS	2.50	
03-00630	ALL HOLIDAYS COOKBOOK	2.50		03-00638	QUICK AND SIMPLE COOKBOOK	2.50	
03-00605	NATURALLY NUTRITIOUS	2.50		03-00603	IDEALS JUNIOR CHEF COOKBOOK	2.50	
03-00609	IDEALS FARMHOUSE COOKBOOK	2.50		03-00711	RECIPE CARD 1	1.00	
03-00641	FROM MAMAS KITCHEN	2.50		03-00712	RECIPE CARD 2	1.00	
03-00626	WHOLE GRAIN COOKBOOK	2.50		06-00716	COOKBOOK VIEWER (LUCITE)	4.00	

SOFT COVER BOOKS 8½ x 11—+5⅜ x 7¼—*4¼ x 7 (R)= (REISSUE)

BK CODE	TITLE	PRICE	QTY	BK CODE	TITLE	PRICE	QTY
04-00046	THE CHRISTMAS MIRACLE	3.95		04-00286	DECORATING FOR THE HOLIDAYS	2.95	
04-00289	LET'S CELEBRATE CHRISTMAS (R)	3.95		04-00288	DESIGNS WITH DRIED FLOWERS	2.95	
04-00051	A FRIEND IS SPECIAL 9/78	3.95		04-00862	TO GOD BE THE GLORY	2.75	
04-00001	THE BEST OF IDEALS 9/78	3.95		04-00376	VEGETABLE GARDENING MADE EASY	2.50	
04-00052	LOOK TO THIS DAY 10/78	3.95		04-00550	BIRD WATCHER'S HANDBOOK +	2.50	
04-00061	GOD LOVES YOU, SO DO I 10/78	3.95		04-00393	A GARDEN OF THOUGHTS	2.25	
04-00059	HOW GREAT THOU ART (R) 10/78	3.95		04-00458	GET WELL WISHES	1.50	
04-00058	IDEALS BEST LOVED POETS 11/78	3.95		04-00462	FAITH FOR TODAY	1.50	
04-00469	CHRISTMAS IS REMEMBERING (R)	2.25		04-00465	HAPPY BIRTHDAY	1.50	
04-00464	THE BEAUTY OF FRIENDSHIP 11/78	1.75		04-00570	HAVE A HAPPY DAY*	1.50	
04-00474	FAVORITE CHRISTMAS CAROLS	1.50		04-00572	MESSAGES OF CHRISTIAN FAITH*	1.50	
04-00574	YOUR LIGHT HAS COME* 11/78	1.50		04-00573	CHEERFUL THOUGHTS AT DAWN*	1.50	
04-00097	THE LORD IS MY SHEPHERD*	1.50					
04-00056	TOUCHED BY THE SEASONS	3.95					

CHILDREN'S BOOKS 8½ x 11—(R)=REISSUE

BK CODE	TITLE	PRICE	QTY	BK CODE	TITLE	PRICE	QTY
04-00055	ONCE UPON A RHYME	3.95		04-00448	JOLLY OLD SANTA CLAUS (R)	2.25	
04-00262	A CHRISTMAS CAROL (R)	2.95		04-00498	THE NIGHT BEFORE CHRISTMAS (R)	1.95	
04-00450	CHRISTMAS FOR CHILDREN	2.25		04-00460	SANTA'S FUN BOOK	1.50	

GIFT BOOKLETS 5⅜ x 7¼—MINIMUM ORDER 6—ANY 10 FOR 5.95

BK CODE	TITLE	PRICE	QTY	BK CODE	TITLE	PRICE	QTY
05-00770	CHRISTMAS GREETINGS	1.00		06-00717	MY DAILY REMINDER	1.00	
05-00798	CHRISTMAS BLESSINGS	1.00		06-00710	CHRISTMAS CARD RECORD BOOK	.75	
05-00769	THANKSGIVING GREETINGS	1.00		05-00760	BIRTHDAY WISHES	.75	
05-00777	YOU ARE MY FRIEND 10/78	1.00		05-00766	A TOUCH OF FRIENDSHIP	.75	
05-00772	TO THE HAPPY PARENTS 10/78	1.00		05-00767	JUST TO SAY THANK YOU	.75	
05-00774	FROM THIS DAY FORWARD 11/78	1.00		05-00794	PLEASE GET WELL	.75	
05-00776	ON YOUR GRADUATION DAY 11/78	1.00		05-00763	WISHING YOU WELL	.75	
				05-00790	WORDS OF INSPIRATION	.75	

HARD COVERS 8½ x 11

BK CODE	TITLE	PRICE	QTY	BK CODE	TITLE	PRICE	QTY
04-00006	IDEALS CHRISTMAS TREASURY	9.95		04-00189	LET'S BE FRIENDS	3.50	
04-00053	HOUSES OF WORSHIP	3.95		04-00670	MESSAGES OF HOPE	2.50	
04-00222	WILDERNESS REFLECTIONS	2.95		04-00685	I FOUND GOD	2.50	

SUB. TOTAL _____

WIS. RES. ONLY ADD 4% TAX (NOT ON SUBS.) _____

POSTAGE AND HANDLING _____

REMIT IN U. S. CURRENCY   TOTAL DUE _____

THANK YOU!

Be sure to recheck your order before mailing to be sure that:

1. You have ordered the right quantity.

2. You have totaled your order accurately.

3. When you have enclosed payment with your order, payment is made in full including shipping charges (and tax where applicable). Please send only U.S. currency. Please do not send cash. Sign all checks and money orders.

4. If your order is OUTSIDE USA that you have included the proper shipping charges with your payment.

5. You have read the postage information in the lower left-hand portion of the order blank.

PLEASE ENTER YOUR NEW ADDRESS HERE:

OLD _____ ZIP CODE _____

NEW _____

D–91

velope and its contents will travel safely through the mail.

FOLD HERE FIRST

IF YOU WISH TO RECEIVE OUR IDEALS CATALOG CHECK HERE. ENTER FRIEND'S NAMES UNDER SPACE PROVIDED OR SEPARATE SHEET.

☐ SEND FUND RAISING INFORMATION

☐ SEND BUSINESS GIFT INFORMATION

D-91

Wisconsin Residents Please Note:
You must Add 4% sales tax on all products sent to Wisconsin addresses, except bimonthly IDEALS issues and subscription to IDEALS bimonthly issues

FOLD SIDE FLAPS FIRST — THEN FOLD HERE

from _____

_____ ZIP CODE _____

ideals PUBLISHING CORPORATION
11315 WATERTOWN PLANK RD.
MILWAUKEE, WISCONSIN 53226

FOR OFFICE USE ONLY

ENTRD		TYPE	KEY	AMT
REMTC		IDEALS	1	
K MO CA				
CHECK FOR ACCURACY		CKBKS	3	
		OTHERS	4	
OVER PAY		GRTS	5	
		BINDERS	8	
		FREIGHT	9	
		SUB-ID	11	
INVOICE AMT		TAX	13	
		POSTAGE	14	

FOLD HERE FIRST

IDENTIFY AS A GIFT FROM _____
TO _____
ADDRESS _____
CITY _____ STATE _____ ZIP _____
MAIL DATE & OCCASION _____

QTY	TITLE	PRICE
	*1 Yr. Subscription (6 issues) to IDEALS	$10.00
	*2 Yr. Subscription (12 issues) to IDEALS	$17.00
	*3 Yr. Subscription (18 issues) to IDEALS	$24.00
	LIST OTHER GIFT SELECTIONS BELOW	
	SEND CATALOG ☐	

IDENTIFY AS A GIFT FROM _____
TO _____
ADDRESS _____
CITY _____ STATE _____ ZIP _____
MAIL DATE & OCCASION _____

QTY	TITLE	PRICE
	*1 Yr. Subscription (6 issues) to IDEALS	$10.00
	*2 Yr. Subscription (12 issues) to IDEALS	$17.00
	*3 Yr. Subscription (18 issues) to IDEALS	$24.00
	LIST OTHER GIFT SELECTIONS BELOW	
	SEND CATALOG ☐	